D1402054

Canada's Political Parties

THE NEW DEMOCRATIC PARTY

Juanita Rossiter

Weigl

Published by Weigl Educational Publishers Limited
6325 10th Street SE
Calgary, Alberta
T2H 2Z9

Website: www.weigl.ca

Library and Archives Canada Cataloguing in Publication Data

Rossiter, Juanita
        New Democratic Party / Juanita Rossiter.

(Canada's political parties)
Includes index.
ISBN 978-1-77071-698-8 (bound) 978-1-77071-703-9 (pbk.)

        1. New Democratic Party. I. Title. II. Series: Canada's political parties (Calgary, Alta.)

JL197.N4R68 2011   j324.27107   C2011-900818-1

Printed in the United States of America in North Mankato, Minnesota
1 2 3 4 5 6 7 8 9 0 15 14 13 12 11

072011
WEP040711

Project Coordinator: Heather Kissock
Design: Terry Paulhus

Photograph Credits
CP Images: pages 6BL, 7, 8, 12, 13TL, 13TR, 14, 15BM, 16, 17BL, 17BR, 18, 19TL, 19TR, 19BR, 20, 21TR, 21BL, 24TL, 24TR, 24M, 25TL, 25M, 25BL; Dreamstime: page 4; Getty Images: pages 6BR, 9TR, 10, 11TL, 11BL, 11BR, 13BL, 13BR, 15TL, 15TR, 15BL, 15BR, 17TL, 17TR, 19BL, 21TL, 21BR, 24TM, 25BR, 26, 27; Glenbow Museum: page 9B, 24B; Library and Archives Canada: pages 9TL, 25TR; Rosetown and District Archives: page 11TL..

Every reasonable effort has been made to trace ownership and to obtain permission to reprint copyright material. The publishers would be pleased to have any errors or omissions brought to their attention so that they may be corrected in subsequent printings.

We acknowledge the financial support of the Government of Canada through the Canada Book Fund for our publishing activities.

CONTENTS

Overview of Canada's Political Parties

Political parties in Canada are made up of people with similar beliefs who have joined together to accomplish specific goals. To achieve these goals, the party attempts to elect enough members to gain control of the government.

Political parties are central to our political system. In their attempts to win elections, parties propose a series of social, economic, and political policies called the party platform. The election campaign then attempts to convince the people to vote for candidates who support these beliefs. This process provides the people with a way of expressing their opinions and of holding the winning party accountable for its actions.

Beginnings

The first Canadian political parties started in central Canada in the 1820s and 1830s. They were created to ensure that the people's wishes were presented to the British governor who ruled the **colonies**. The achievement of **responsible government** in the late 1840s paved the way for the emergence of party politics as we know it today. When Canada became a nation in 1867, there was only the Liberal Party and the Conservative Party. These two parties dominated politics until the 1920s. The rise of the Progressive Party in the 1920s, and the emergence of the Co-operative Commonwealth Federation (CCF) and the Social Credit parties in the 1930s gave voters more choices through which to express their concerns. However, these "third" parties never seriously challenged the power of the two major parties.

This situation changed, however, in the 1980s. The Reform Party began in 1987 as an alternative to the Progressive Conservative Party. In 2000, it transformed into the Canadian Alliance, which then merged with the Progressive Conservative Party in 2003 to form the Conservative Party of Canada. Today, the Conservative Party, Liberal Party, New Democratic Party (NDP), Green Party, and Bloc Québécois compete to dominate Canadian Politics.

🍁 The Parliament Buildings in Ottawa have been the centre of Canadian politics since 1867.

The New Democratic Party—
Its Beliefs and Philosophy

The New Democratic Party is a progressive political party with a social democratic philosophy. Social democracy is a term that is generally used by individuals on the **political left** to describe their beliefs. Social democrats believe in using established political processes to bring about changes to **capitalism** so that poverty and inequality are eliminated. The NDP, and its predecessor the CCF, have been the political parties in Canada that have most consistently expressed a social democratic vision.

Policy Statements

The New Democratic Party's vision for Canada is rooted in "economic prosperity and social equality for all Canadians." Some of the NDP's key beliefs and policy statements are as follows:

- The NDP believes that economic prosperity for all Canadians can be achieved through proper regulation and strategic investments in the country's physical and social **infrastructure**.

- The NDP's social policy is based on the goal of building a society in which all of its members can reach their full potential. This is achieved in part by protecting the vulnerable and ensuring that every citizen has access to high-quality social programs and by advocating for continued improvements in **Medicare**.

- On the international front, the NDP believes that Canada has an obligation to share its wealth with the world's most poor and vulnerable. It must become a leader for food security, women's equality, ensuring environmental sustainability, and ending the AIDS pandemic.

Registering a Political Party

1. Political parties do not have to be registered with the government. However, registered parties can provide tax receipts for donations, thus saving the donors money. An official party can place its name beneath its candidates' names on the ballot.

2. To be registered, a party must:
- Have statements from at least 250 individuals who are qualified to vote (i.e. 18 years old and a Canadian citizen) indicating that they are party members
- Endorse at least one candidate in a general election or a by-election
- Have at least three officers, in addition to the party leader, who live in Canada and are eligible to vote
- Have an auditor
- Submit a copy of the party's resolution appointing its leader
- Have an agent who is qualified to sign contracts
- Submit a letter stating that the party will support one or more of its members as candidates for election

3. The party's name, abbreviation, or logo must not resemble those of any other party and must not include the word "independent." Once the Chief Electoral Officer has verified the party's application (confirming that 250 electors are members of the party and that the party has met all the other requirements), and is satisfied that the party's name and logo will not be confused with those of another registered or eligible party, he or she will inform the party leader that the party is eligible for registration.

Source: Elections Canada

New Democratic Party Leaders

The New Democratic Party has never formed a government at the federal level. However, its influence has been felt across Canada and is most apparent in many of the social programs currently operating in the country. Throughout its short history, the leaders of the NDP have fought with determination to achieve the party's goals.

New Democratic Party Leaders

NAME	TERM
Tommy Douglas	1961-1971
David Lewis	1971-1975
Ed Broadbent	1975-1989
Audrey McLaughlin	1989-1995
Alexa McDonough	1995-2003
Jack Layton	2003-

FIRST PARTY LEADER

TOMMY DOUGLAS (1904–1986)

Douglas was born in Falkirk, Scotland. His family initially immigrated to Canada in 1910 and settled in Winnipeg. However, they returned to Scotland during World War I, not returning to Canada until 1919. In 1924, Douglas began studying theology at Brandon College. He graduated in 1930 and then went on to complete a master's degree in sociology at McMaster University. During World War II, he enlisted in the Canadian Army. He later went on to become the 7th premier of Saskatchewan, the first leader of the NDP, and a member of the House of Commons. Tommy Douglas is most remembered for introducing universal health care legislation.

SECOND PARTY LEADER

DAVID LEWIS 1909–1981)

Lewis was born in Svisloch, Russia. His father Moishe Losh immigrated to Canada in 1921. Within a few months, he had saved up enough money to send for his family. Lewis' first language was Yiddish, but he quickly learned English and went on to study at McGill University. He later won a Rhodes Scholarship to Oxford University in London, England. In addition to his political life, Lewis worked as a labour lawyer and was a professor at Carleton University.

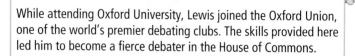

While attending Oxford University, Lewis joined the Oxford Union, one of the world's premier debating clubs. The skills provided here led him to become a fierce debater in the House of Commons.

Tommy Douglas is often referred to as the Father of Medicare for his contribution to universal health care in Canada.

ED BROADBENT
(1936–)

Broadbent was born in Oshawa, Ontario. For a brief period in the 1980s, Broadbent was the most popular politician in Canada. He scored higher in public opinion polls than then Prime Minister Pierre Trudeau. Broadbent has a Ph.D. in political science from the University of Toronto, was a member of the Royal Canadian Air Force, and eventually became a professor at Queen's University. Some of the issues Broadbent fought for were an equitable tax system, equality for women, and Aboriginal and economic rights.

Broadbent made a brief return to federal politics in 2004, becoming the member of Parliament (MP) for Ottawa Centre. He left this position the following year when his wife became ill.

AUDREY MCLAUGHLIN
(1936–)

McLaughlin was born in Dutton, Ontario. Before entering politics, she had a number of careers. These included work as a farmer, teacher, small business operator, and community worker. McLaughlin has a master's degree in social work from the University of Toronto, and has worked as a social worker in Toronto and Ghana, Africa. In the late 1970s, she moved to the Yukon and set up a consulting business. McLaughlin began her political career in 1987 when she became the first federal NDP candidate to win in the Yukon. Since leaving politics, she has worked on social issues in Canada and around the world.

Audrey McLaughlin has been made an Officer of the Order of Canada for her work in the area of social justice.

ALEXA MCDONOUGH
(1944–)

McDonough was born in Ottawa in 1944. Her father, Lloyd Shaw, served as the first research director for the CCF. Involved in social activism from an early age, McDonough was 14 years old when she led her church youth group in publicizing the conditions of Africville, a low-income African-Canadian neighbourhood in Halifax. She worked as a social worker before entering politics in 1979. Upon retirement from politics, McDonough was appointed president of Mount Saint Vincent University, in Halifax, Nova Scotia.

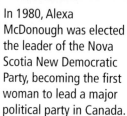

In 1980, Alexa McDonough was elected the leader of the Nova Scotia New Democratic Party, becoming the first woman to lead a major political party in Canada.

JACK LAYTON
(1950–)

Layton was born in Montréal and raised in Hudson, Québec. Layton went on to become a professor at Ryerson University, an author, a prominent activist, and a member of the Toronto City Council before becoming federal leader of the NDP. Layton comes from a long line of politicians. His great-grandfather was a blind activist who led a campaign for disability pensions in the 1930s; his grandfather, Gilbert Layton, was a cabinet minister in Québec; his father, Robert Layton served as a Progressive Conservative member of Parliament (MP) and Cabinet minister in the 1980s.

Jack Layton received his Ph.D. in political science from Toronto's York University in 1983.

🍁 The Great Depression was a time of great frustration throughout the country. In 1935, men from across Western Canada rode freight trains to Ottawa to protest poor-paying government work projects.

Party Origins, 1909–1932

The New Democratic Party has its origins in the Co-operative Commonwealth Federation (CCF) that was founded in Calgary, Alberta, in 1932. The CCF was formed to work toward improving the lives of Canadians suffering the effects of the **Great Depression**.

Many Canadian farmers had been angry and frustrated with the government since World War I. Following the war, the world market for wheat collapsed and many prairie farmers were desperately short of cash. Farmers had been encouraged to mechanize during the war in order to increase production, and now they faced large debts. The farmers' movement grew, and political parties 'dedicated to the farmers' cause, such as the United Farmers and the Progressive Party, rose to prominence.

As the Great Depression gained a grip on the nation, these parties began to decline. Some members moved to the Liberal Party, while others began searching for a new way for their voices to be heard.

Some radical Progressives went on to form a faction called The Ginger Group. This group, along with labour and farmer organizations, eventually helped form the CCF.

The CCF was influenced greatly by The League for Social Reconstruction (LSR). This group was founded in 1931 by academics who advocated social and economic reforms and political education. It worked with both intellectuals and politicians to address problems resulting from the Depression.

The goal of the LSR was to motivate Canadians to critically examine Canada's political economy. The LSR believed that the existing political system was not practical, and it instead advocated a socialist government. The League felt that the Great Depression was caused by a capitalistic economy, and that a permanent solution could only be found in democratic **socialism**.

Many Canadian farmers had been angry and frustrated with the government since World War I.

WHO SHOULD REPRESENT THE FARMERS?

After World War I, voters in Western Canada were left with no party loyalties. The farmers' movement had to decide how to get their message to the voting public. Would it be best to enlist Liberal candidates to represent their point of view, or would the farmers' movement have more success running political candidates of its own?

LIBERAL

After losing support in the 1917 election, the Liberals had to rebuild their party. Aligning themselves with the farmers' movement would bring them much-needed support in the West. The farmers' movement supported free trade with the U.S., which had also been advocated by previous Liberal governments. The Liberals feared, however, that they would lose support from Québec if they supported the farmers' movement.

FARMERS

The conditions were right for the rise of an independent political movement. Popular support for an independent party representing the interests of western Canadians spread quickly.

THE RESULT

The farmers' movement, along with the Canadian Council of Agriculture, started running candidates in by-elections in late 1919. By 1920, they were committed to independent political action. That year, Thomas Crerar, the former Minister of Agriculture in Conservative Prime Minister Robert Borden's government, and 10 other MPs formed the National Progressive Party. The party emerged as a voice for the farmers' movement.

Beginning with the United Farmers of Alberta in 1909, farmers in many provinces established their own political parties. Over time, the United Farmers movement spread to almost every province in the country.

- United Farmers of British Columbia (Established in 1917)
- United Farmers of Alberta (Established in 1909)
- United Farmers of Canada (Saskatchewan section) (Established in 1926)
- United Farmers of Ontario (Established in 1914)
- United Farmers of New Brunswick (Established in 1918)
- United Farmers of Québec (Established in 1920)
- United Farmers of Nova Scotia (Established in 1920)
- United Farmers of Prince Edward Island (Established in 1920)

The United Farmers of Alberta began as a lobby group but eventually became a political party. It governed Alberta from 1921 to 1935.

The CCF Years, 1932–1961

After forming in 1932, the CCF held a party convention the next year in Regina, Saskatchewan. It was here that the party's program was formally adopted. The Regina **Manifesto** stressed the need for society to look at human needs rather than making profits. It vowed to eradicate capitalism as part of its **mandate**.

The CCF had immediate support in Western Canada, where it quickly became the official opposition in British Columbia and Saskatchewan. By 1943, the CCF had moved eastward, becoming the official opposition in the Ontario legislature. A year later, the Saskatchewan CCF won the provincial election and made history by forming the first socialist government in North America with Tommy Douglas as premier.

The CCF reached the height of its membership in the mid 1940s. However, after World War II, party membership began to decline. In 1956, party leaders tried to regain members by replacing the Regina Manifesto with the Winnipeg Declaration. The Winnipeg Declaration differed from the Regina Manifesto in that it called for a mixed economy in which there were clearly visible roles for public, private, and co-operative enterprise working together in the people's interest. The effort did not bring about the change the CCF were looking for, and, in the 1958 federal election, the CCF only won eight seats.

This decline in the polls led to a merger between the CCF and the Canadian Labour Congress (CLC). In 1958, a joint CCF-CLC committee, the National Committee for the New Party (NCNP), was formed. The aim of the NCNP Committee was to create a new social democratic political party. The NCNP committee spent three years establishing the foundations for this new political party. Finally, in 1961, a national convention was held in Ottawa, Ontario. At this convention, the structure and principles of the New Democratic Party were established.

> The CCF had immediate support in Western Canada.

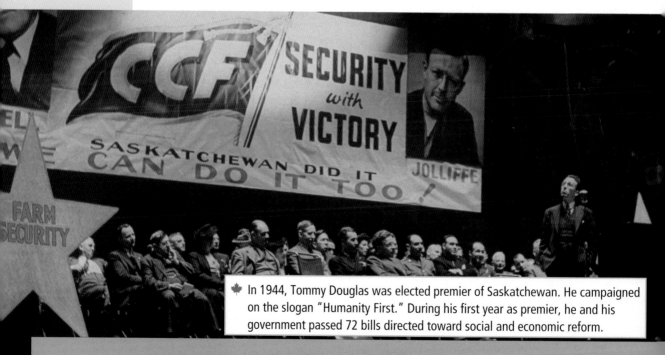

In 1944, Tommy Douglas was elected premier of Saskatchewan. He campaigned on the slogan "Humanity First." During his first year as premier, he and his government passed 72 bills directed toward social and economic reform.

SHOULD THE CCF REMAIN AUTONOMOUS?

The CCF's decision to merge with the Canadian Labour Congress involved much discussion. There were advantages and disadvantages to aligning the goals of the CCF with another organization. Some questioned whether it would be better to remain an autonomous party.

REMAIN AUTONOMOUS

MERGE

Merging with the CLC would mean compromise on some level. The radical platform of the CCF would inevitably shift to a more moderate-left reform position. If the CCF remained autonomous, it would not need to worry about any of its core values being lost in an updated party.

Due to its left-wing ideologies, the CCF was often accused of having **communist** leanings. Aligning with the CLC would strengthen the party and bring it closer to mainstream thinking. The CCF also felt that merging with the CLC, an established labour organization, would make social democracy more popular with Canadians.

THE RESULT

In 1958, the CLC and the CCF joined forces and created a 20-person joint committee, the National Committee for the New Party (NCNP), to discuss the foundation of a new political party. Three years of negotiations and talks resulted in the founding of the New Democratic Party in 1961.

The Regina Manifesto laid out several goals the CCF hoped to achieve. Among these goals were:

1. **Universal** pensions, universal health care, and children's benefits
2. Unemployment insurance, a national labour code, and workers compensation
3. Public ownership of key industries
4. More social rights, including equal treatment of all Canadians before the law no matter what race, nationality, religion, or political beliefs

Children's allowances were intended to subsidize parents for the cost of raising a child.

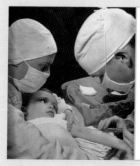

Universal health care was a key cause for the NDP. They believed that all Canadians should have the same access to medical care.

The formation of the NDP united the CCF and the labour movement. When Tommy Douglas was elected the party's first leader, representatives from the CCF and labour unions were some of the first to congratulate him.

Emergence of the NDP, 1961–1975

The New Democratic Party was officially founded on June 17, 1961. Tommy Douglas, the former CCF premier of Saskatchewan, was elected the first federal NDP leader.

The party's first federal election was a difficult one for Douglas. Emerging as the political voice of Canadian Labour, the NDP only won 19 seats in 1962, and Douglas lost his own seat. In order to stay a member of the House of Commons, Douglas had to run in a by-election in the British Columbia riding of Burnaby-Coquitlam.

The party was unable to gain much support throughout the 1960s, and in 1971, Douglas resigned as leader of the NDP. He was replaced by former party president David Lewis.

Lewis came from a family with strong political roots. In the 1972 federal election, he led the NDP to its largest number of seats won to that date. With 31 members in the House of Commons, the NDP held the balance of power in Pierre Trudeau's Liberal **minority government**.

Although the two parties never entered into a coalition, the NDP worked with the Liberal government in the mid 1970s to introduce progressive programs into law. However, in 1974, they formed an alliance with the Progressive Conservatives to bring down the Liberal government in a **vote of non-confidence**.

The election that followed did not provide the NDP with an increase in seats, however. This time, Trudeau and his Liberal party won a majority government. This majority came at the expense of the NDP, which lost half its seats and elected only 16 candidates. David Lewis was one of the people who lost his seat and therefore resigned as leader. The following year, Ed Broadbent secured the NDP leadership.

Tommy Douglas, the former CCF premier of Saskatchewan, was elected the first federal NDP leader.

THE WAFFLE IN THE NDP

During the 1971 leadership convention, David Lewis campaigned against James Laxer, the leader of a group within the NDP known as the Waffle. Established in 1969, the Waffle represented the radical left wing of the NDP. The group called for an independent socialist Canada. Even though Lewis won the party leadership, the Waffle continued to exert its extreme ideas on the party. The NDP had to decide if it would let the Waffle remain part of the party establishment, which would ultimately push the NDP further left on the political spectrum.

KEEP THE WAFFLE

The Waffle's platform called for a return to basic socialist principals. Many members of the NDP, including future party leader Ed Broadbent, supported the Waffle's stance against American **imperialism** and foreign ownership, and support for Québec's right to self government. In 1971, approximately 2,000 of the NDP's 90,000 members were members of the Waffle. Forcing the Waffle out of the NDP therefore threatened to alienate many NDP party members.

NO TO THE WAFFLE

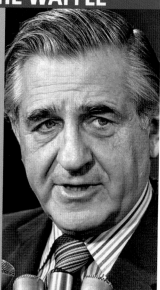

The Waffle was part of the NDP, but its commitment to day-to-day activism made it seem more like an independent movement. The Waffle and its *Manifesto for an Independent Socialist Canada* caused division in the party. As a result, there was much party infighting.

THE RESULT

Members of the party establishment and the trade union delegation voted down the Waffle's resolutions in 1972, and the party pressured the Waffle to either disband or leave the NDP. Waffle members quit the NDP and formed the Movement for an Independent Socialist Canada. This group disbanded in 1974.

Liberal Cooperation

Together, the NDP and the Liberals brought the following programs and institutions to Canadians.
1. A national affordable housing strategy
2. A new Elections Expenses Act
3. Petro-Canada, created as Canada's national oil and gas company
4. The **Foreign Investment Review Agency**

NDP leader David Lewis worked closely with Prime Minister Pierre Trudeau to create a national affordable housing program so that people from all walks of life could have a roof over their heads.

The goal in creating Petro-Canada was to allow Canadians across the country to benefit from the sale of oil.

A Time to Grow, 1979–1988

In 1979, the Progressive Conservative (PC) Party won the federal election under the leadership of Joe Clark. Soon into its new term, Clark's government was under attack. At first, Joe Clark's inexperience was an issue. Then, John Crosbie, the Minister of Finance, introduced a controversial budget that contradicted Conservative campaign promises. Under the leadership of Ed Broadbent, the NDP played a critical role in moving the motion of non-confidence on Crosbie's budget. The motion brought down the PC government. In the election that followed, the Liberals returned to power.

In 1983, the NDP decided to move the party back to the political left with more of a focus on regional problems. To do this, it replaced the 1956 Winnipeg Declaration with the Statement of Principles. The Statement reiterated the NDP's social democratic stance by rejecting capitalist theories and promoting **decentralized** ownership.

The new direction gave the NDP a boost in public support. While the 1984 federal election saw the PC party win the most seats in Canadian history, it also witnessed the NDP win 30 seats. The NDP had won only 10 seats fewer than the Liberals.

The NDP continued on this wave of success in the 1988 federal election, with a total of 43 members of Parliament elected. Although it was the party's strongest showing, Broadbent faced criticism within the party for not focussing his campaign on the party's opposition to the Canada–United States **Free Trade** Agreement. His support of the **Meech Lake Accord** also met with disapproval. In 1989, Broadbent stepped down after being the NDP leader for 14 years.

> In 1983, the NDP decided to move the party back to the political left with more of a focus on regional problems.

🍁 Following the 1979 leaders' debate, polls indicated that many Canadians felt Ed Broadbent had the strongest showing. This did not stop Joe Clark and his Conservative Party from winning a minority government in the election that followed.

DEFEATING THE GOVERNMENT

Minister of Finance, John Crosbie, introduced a budget in December 1979 that was immediately criticized for including tax increases, and, in particular, an 18-cent-a-gallon gasoline tax. The NDP had to decide if it would support the Liberals' vote of non-confidence and bring down the Conservative government.

YES

NDP finance critic Bob Rae described Crosbie's budget as the "budget that stole Christmas." The PC budget included tax increases that would affect all Canadians. NDP leader Ed Broadbent stated that they "had a Prime Minister for the last seven months who hasn't listened to the people of Canada."

NO

Introducing a motion of non-confidence would result in two federal elections in less than a year. Canadians were dealing with the impact of high inflation, rising unemployment and an economic deficit. Another election would result in more taxpayer dollars spent and possible resentment for the political parties responsible for initiating the election.

THE RESULT

The NDP and the Liberal Party passed a vote of non-confidence, and the Conservative government was forced to resign. The ensuing 1980 election returned the Liberal Party under Pierre Trudeau to power. The NDP won 32 seats.

Statement of Principals

The 1983 Statement of Principles was divided into four sections.

1. Our Ends, which expressed the need for societal improvements
2. Our Means, which expressed its belief in the need for systemic government change
3. Our Historical Task, which committed the party to repairing the environment
4. Commitment to Canada, which encouraged active participation in Canadian society

The Statement of Principles expressed the NDP's belief that Canada's Aboriginal community had the right to shape its own future.

The Statement of Principles reaffirmed the party's traditional stance on decentralized ownership and its support of co-operatives and credit unions.

The need to protect the environment and use it effectively is a key component of the Statement of Principles.

While McDonough was believed to be shifting the NDP to the centre of the political spectrum, the party's election platform remained focussed on traditional NDP concerns.

A Party in Decline, 1989–2000

In July of 1987, Audrey McLaughlin was elected to the House of Commons as the MP for the Yukon. Two years later, she was elected as leader of the NDP. This made her the first female leader of a political party with representation in the Canadian House of Commons.

McLaughlin began her term as national leader at the height of NDP popularity. Shortly after she began, however, the party experienced a steady decline in the polls. This was partially due to the rise of the Reform Party in Western Canada as well as the poor performance of NDP provincial governments in British Columbia and Ontario. These factors led to a devastating loss for the party in the 1993 federal election. The NDP was left with only nine seats in Parliament. This was three seats short of what was needed for official party status in the House of Commons. McLaughlin won her seat in the Yukon, but resigned as party leader in 1994.

McLaughlin was replaced by Alexa McDonough, who had been the leader of the Nova Scotia New Democratic Party from 1980 to 1994. McDonough was able to make up for lost ground. In the 1997 election, the NDP increased its elected members from 9 to 21. This breakthrough, however, was quickly followed by a few years of controversy for McDonough and the NDP.

One of the main issues in the party during these years was McDonough's plans for the party. Many felt that she was trying to move the party to the centre of the **political spectrum**. Another challenge for the federal NDP at this time was the presence of the Canadian Alliance under its new leader Stockwell Day. NDP supporters who feared the prospect of a Canadian Alliance government moved their support to the Liberal Party.

McLaughlin became leader of the NDP, making her the first female leader of a political party with representation in the Canadian House of Commons.

CAMPAIGN PLANNING

After the NDP's success in the 1988 election, it began a period of decline. Under new leader Audrey McLaughlin, the NDP had to decide where to focus the party's efforts in the 1993 federal election campaign to increase its seats in parliament. Would the party do best to campaign strongly in Eastern or Western Canada?

EAST

In 1989, the Québec New Democratic Party took on a **sovereigntist** platform and broke away from the federal NDP. The NDP wanted to re-establish a working relationship with Québec. In 1990, the NDP won its first seat ever in the province. Focussing attention on Québec might result in additional elected candidates.

WEST

The Reform Party had emerged and quickly developed an extensive network in Western Canada. It struck a chord with many western NDP supporters and threatened to take votes from the NDP. Although Western Canada was considered the heartland of the NDP, the party ran the risk of being alienated if it ignored its traditional supporters.

THE RESULT

Instead of focussing on Western alienation, Audrey McLaughlin focussed on expanding NDP support in Québec. This did not work. The NDP lost the one seat it had gained in 1990. The NDP won only nine seats, while the Reform Party experienced a substantial breakthrough in the 1993 federal election.

Provincial Success

While the NDP has never achieved a federal leadership position, it has succeeded in forming several provincial governments.

1. Saskatchewan and Manitoba have had more NDP governments than other provinces. Saskatchewan has had an NDP government seven times, while Manitoba has had eight NDP governments.
2. British Columbia has had three NDP governments.
3. Ontario, Nova Scotia, and the Yukon have each had one NDP government.

Although he became a Liberal MP, Ujjal Dosanjh was once a member of the NDP. While with the NDP, he served as premier of British Columbia.

Gary Doer was the premier of Manitoba from 1999 to 2009. In 2009, Prime Minister Stephen Harper appointed Doer to the position of Ambassador to the United States.

Years of Renewal, 2000–2002

The 2000 federal election saw the Liberal Party win a majority government. The NDP focussed its campaign on the issue of Medicare, but lost significant support. The party slipped in both votes and seats, only electing 13 MPs and winning 8.5 percent of the popular vote. The disappointing results were near its historic low in the 1993 election. The difference was that in the 2000 election the party was able to maintain official party status in the House of Commons.

The results of the 2000 election led to calls within the NDP for party renewal. Some party members felt that the NDP had moved too far to the centre of the political spectrum. In an effort to change this, two movements were initiated by NDP members, NDProgress and the New Politics Initiative (NPI). Each had its own ideas regarding the future of the NDP.

The goal of NDProgress was to increase the electoral success of the NDP by reforming the internal structure of the party. NDProgress suggested changes to how leaders were elected and sought to limit the control labour unions had in the party. Both of these suggestions met with success at future party conventions.

The New Politics Initiative (NPI) was founded in 2002, one year after the NDProgress was formed, and was supported by several high-profile party members. They felt the NDP was close to becoming another Liberal Party and called for the NDP to disband. NPI supporters wanted to form another political party under a different name. The 2001 Winnipeg convention saw the NPI's proposal defeated. The group formally dissolved in 2004.

The 2001 national NDP convention in Winnipeg witnessed significant changes to the structure of the NDP, with it adopting several of the NDProgress suggestions. With these changes, the party reaffirmed to its members the NDP commitment to the political left.

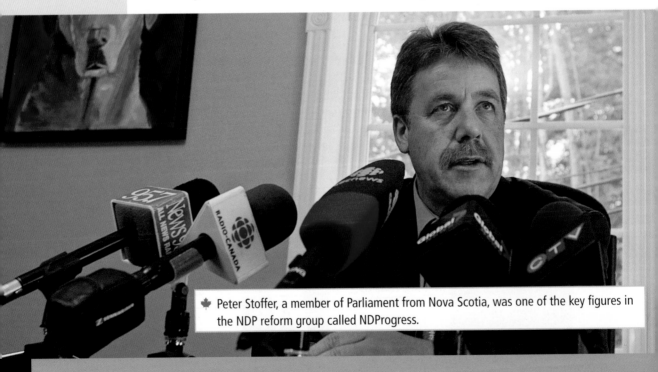

❦ Peter Stoffer, a member of Parliament from Nova Scotia, was one of the key figures in the NDP reform group called NDProgress.

SHOULD THE NDP DISBAND?

Following the disappointing result of the 2000 federal election, the NDProgress supporters called for renewal and party reform. The NPI, however, felt that it was time to disband the party and create something new in its place. The issue caused much discussion within party ranks.

REFORM

NDProgress felt that the electoral success of the NDP could be increased by reforming the internal structure of the party. It advocated limiting the control labour unions had in the party and believed that the party could be further strengthened by changing how its leaders were elected.

DISBAND

The NPI, which included Svend Robinson and Judy Rebick, saw strength in uniting Canada's political left. It believed the NDP to be more than Canada's labour voice. The NPI felt that left-wing activists could be attracted to the NDP if it adopted more left-wing ideas. The NPI advocated forming another political party under a different name and called for the NDP to disband.

THE RESULT

The NPI's proposals were defeated at the 2001 Winnipeg convention. Alexa McDonough endorsed the NDProgress recommendation of a "**one member one party**" voting system, which entailed selecting party leaders and determining party policy by a direct vote of party members. At the convention, the NDProgess was also effective in having a resolution passed that limited union and corporate donations.

Founded in 2000, the NDProgress called for five reforms.

1. The introduction of a one member one party voting system to elect the party leader
2. Placing a ban on union and corporate donations to the party
2. Changing the party's relationship with the Canadian Labour Congress
3. Separating the provincial and federal wings of the party
4. Changing the party name

While corporate and union donations were not banned, the NDProgress were able to claim victory, when in 2003, the NDP resolved to limit this type of financing.

Alexa McDonough supported the concept of one member one party voting at an NDP conference in 2001. This allows for every member to have an individual vote. In the past, all of the members of a constituency had to elect a delegate to vote on their behalf.

🍁 In the 2011 election, Jack Layton led the NDP to its best showing ever, winning 30.62 percent of the vote. The party became the Official Opposition for the first time in history.

The Contemporary Era, 2002–2011

In the 2008 federal election, the NDP increased its numbers in the House of Commons.

Alexa McDonough stepped down as party leader in 2003, and Jack Layton was elected the new federal NDP leader the following January. When an election was called in 2004, the Liberals were re-elected with a minority government. The election produced mixed results for the NDP. Layton had aimed to reach at least 43 seats, but the NDP gained only five seats, for a total of 19 elected members. As had been the case in the minority governments in the 1970s, the NDP found themselves in a position to trade support on issues with the Liberal minority. These included fighting the **privatization** of health care and working to meet Canada's obligation to the **Kyoto Protocol**.

The 2006 federal election was prompted by a motion of non-confidence made by Conservative leader Stephen Harper. This time, the Conservatives won a minority government. The NDP won a total of 29 seats. What was also significant about the 2006 election results is that 41 percent of elected NDP members were women. This marked the highest proportion of women that had ever existed in a Canadian parliamentary **caucus** with official party status.

In the 2008 federal election, the NDP increased its numbers in the House of Commons. Winning 37 seats brought the NDP the third most seats won since the 1988 election, when it won 43 seats.

The 2011 federal election was historic for the NDP. The party won the largest number of seats in its history and became the official opposition in the House of Commons for the first time, with 103 elected members. The NDP also made firm inroads in Québec, electing 59 MPs when they had previously only ever elected two candidates.

REVOKING THE CLARITY ACT

In the 2004 campaign, NDP leader Jack Layton proposed the removal of the Clarity Act, a law that set out the rules under which a province could **secede** from Canada. The Liberal government had enacted the law following the 1995 **Québec Referendum**. It was designed to ensure that the federal government had input when a province wanted to separate from **Confederation**. Layton's proposal was controversial within his party and across the country. Some Canadians thought that the act was vital to keep Québec in Canada, while others believed that it was undemocratic. The issue divided the party.

REVOKE

Jack Layton felt that the Clarity Act had not been helpful in the debate over Québec sovereignty. He felt it had done nothing for national unity. Instead, Layton felt the Act had accentuated divisions in Canada.

KEEP

When the Clarity Act was passed in 2000, the NDP supported it. High profile NDP members, including Alexa McDonough, stood behind the Act. Without it, there was a chance Québec would separate from Canada if another referendum was to take place.

THE RESULT

Layton's efforts to reach out to voters in Québec were unsuccessful. In the 2004 election, the Liberals were re-elected with a minority government. The NDP only gained five seats, for a total of 19 elected members. In the 2006 election campaign, Layton reversed his position on the Clarity Act.

NDP Legacy

The NDP and its predecessor, the CCF, have brought social democratic thought to the Canadian mainstream. In Canada, the social democratic platform has encouraged the initiation of legislation such as:

1. Family Allowances
2. Workers' Compensation
3. Unemployment Insurance
4. Minimum wage
5. Old age pensions

Employment insurance provides financial assistance to people who have lost their jobs.

Today, family allowances have been replaced with the Child Tax benefit. The program provides up to $85 per month per child, depending on the family's income.

TIMELINE

Even though the NDP is one of Canada's younger political parties, it has contributed much to the country. Whether directly or indirectly, the party's social democratic platform has given Canada many of its present-day social programs. The following timeline indicates the events that led to the creation of the NDP and its growth as a party.

1901

1929

Canada's farmers' movement begins.

The Great Depression hits Canada.

1931–32

The League for Social Reconstruction (LSR) is founded.

1932

The Co-operative Commonwealth Federation (CCF) forms.

1933

The CCF drafts its Regina Manifesto.

1935

Seven CCF candidates are elected to the House of Commons.

1943–44

The CCF becomes the official opposition in the Ontario legislature.

1944

Tommy Douglas is elected premier of Saskatchewan.

1956

The Winnipeg Declaration replaces the Regina Manifesto.

1958

The National Committee for the New Party (NCNP) is formed.

1961

The New Democratic Party (NDP) is formed. Tommy Douglas is the party's first leader.

1971

David Lewis is elected leader of the federal NDP.

1975

Ed Broadbent becomes the federal NDP leader.

1983

The Statement of Principles replaces the Winnipeg Declaration.

1989

Ed Broadbent steps down after being leader for 14 years.

1989

Audrey McLaughlin becomes the federal NDP leader.

1993

The NDP win only nine seats in the federal election and lose their official party status.

1994

Alexa McDonough becomes the federal NDP leader.

1997

The NDP has a breakthrough in Atlantic Canada, taking two seats from Liberal ministers in the federal election.

2000

The NDProgress is established.

2001

The New Politics Initiative is established.

2003

Jack Layton becomes the federal NDP leader.

2011

The NDP become the Official Opposition in the House of Commons.

10 FAST FACTS
ABOUT THE NEW DEMOCRATIC PARTY

1 In 2004, CBC's *The Greatest Canadian* television program named Tommy Douglas the "Greatest Canadian."

2 Jack Layton's great-granduncle William Steeves was a Father of Confederation.

3 The NDP was the first major party to elect a woman MP as its leader. This occurred in 1989 when Audrey McLaughlin became party leader.

4 Before coming to Canada, Tommy Douglas fell and injured his right knee. In Canada, doctors told his parents that Tommy's leg would have to be amputated. Fortunately, a well-known orthopedic surgeon offered to treat him for free if his parents would allow medical students to observe. Douglas's leg was saved. This experience convinced him that health care should be free to all. "I felt that no boy should have to depend either for his leg or his life upon the ability of his parents to raise enough money to bring a first-class surgeon to his bedside," he said.

5 The Regina Manifesto, created during J.S. Woodsworth's term as leader, scared many people with its Marxist language. "No CCF government will rest content until it has eradicated capitalism and put into operation the full programme of socialized planning ...," it read.

6 David Lewis's family had a long tradition of socialist politics. His father was a socialist supporter in Russia. David's eldest son, Stephen, led the Ontario NDP from 1970 until 1978. In 1971, David and Stephen became one of the first father-and-son-teams to simultaneously head Canadian political parties.

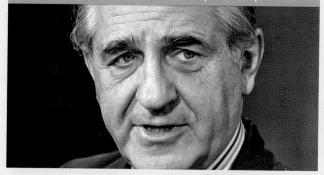

7 In 1943, David Lewis and the CCF's National Chairman, F. R. Scott, wrote *Make This Your Canada: A Review of CCF History and Policy.* The book sold more than 25,000 copies in its first year.

8 In May 1987, public opinion polls revealed that the NDP had more support from Canadians than either the Liberal or Conservative parties.

9 Since its founding, the federal NDP has obtained an average 15.4 percent of the vote.

10 The success of the NDP in Québec following the 2011 election was nicknamed the "orange crush." Orange is the official NDP colour.

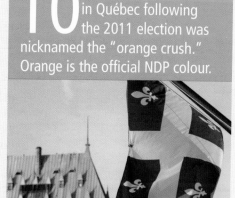

ACTIVITY

WHAT IS A DEBATE?

When people debate a topic, two sides take a different viewpoint about one idea. They present logical arguments to support their views. Usually, each person or team is given a set amount of time to present its case. The presenters take turns stating their arguments until the total time set aside for the debate is used up. Sometimes, there is an audience in the room listening to the presentations. Later, the members of the audience vote for the person or team they think made the most persuasive arguments.

Debating is an important skill. It helps people to think about ideas thoughtfully and carefully. It also helps them develop rhythms of speech that others can follow easily.

Some schools have organized debating clubs as part of their after-school activities. Schools often hold debates in their history class or as part of studying about world events.

DEBATE THIS!

Every day, the news is filled with the issues facing Canada and its citizens. These issues are debated in the House of Commons and on city streets. People often have different views of these issues and support different solutions.

Following is an issue that has sparked discussion across the country. Gather your friends or classmates, and divide into two teams to debate the issue. Each team should take time to properly research the issue and develop solid arguments for their side.

Taking care of the environment is an integral part of the NDP's mandate. They have supported the Kyoto Protocol, and have encouraged Canada to be "green." Some of Canada's major industries rely on products that are not "green." A significant portion of Canada's oil and gas industry, for instance, is based on fossil fuels. Burning these fuels is not considered a green practice. It is using a non-renewable resource that is sending pollutants into the air.

Should the Canadian government ban the manufacture and use of fossil fuels in favour of more green energy sources?

QUIZ

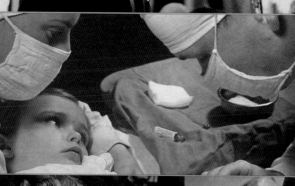

1. What philosophy is behind the NDP's platform?

2. What does CCF stand for?

3. What is Tommy Douglas best known for?

4. List three goals found in the Regina Manifesto.

5. Who replaced Tommy Douglas as NDP leader?

6. What document replaced the Winnipeg Declaration?

7. Which NDP leader was the first woman to lead a political party with representation in the Canadian House of Commons?

8. What were the two NDP programs that arose in the 2000s to encourage party change?

9. What percentage of elected party members were women in the 2006 election?

10. How many provinces have had an NDP government?

FURTHER RESEARCH

Suggested Reading

Archer, Keith. *Political Activists: The NDP in Convention*. Toronto: Oxford University Press Canada, 1997.

McLeod, Ian. *Under Siege: The Federal NDP in the Nineties*. Toronto: James Lorimer and Company Ltd., 1994

Whitehorn, Alan. *Canadian Socialism: Essays on the CCF-NDP*. Toronto: Oxford University Press, 1992.

Internet Resources

Read about the New Democratic Party directly from the source at **www.ndp.ca**

A detailed history of the New Democratic Party can be found at **www.thecanadianencyclopedia.com**. Just type NDP into the search bar.

Learn more about Canada's political parties and the election process at **www.elections.ca**

GLOSSARY

capitalism: an economic system in which investment in and ownership of the means of production, distribution, and exchange of wealth is made and maintained chiefly by private individuals or corporations

caucus: a closed meeting of a group of persons belonging to the same political party or faction, usually to select candidates or to decide on policy

colonies: regions ruled by a country that is usually far away

communist: relating to a social organization based on the holding of all property in common, actual ownership being ascribed to the community as a whole or to the state

Confederation: the event in 1867 when Canada became its own country

decentralized: distributed the administrative functions of a central authority among several local authorities

Foreign Investment Review Agency: a federal organization that reviews concerns about foreign presence in the Canadian economy

free trade: trading between countries without taxes, duties, or restrictions

Great Depression: a period in the 1930s which was characterized by high unemployment and low sales of products

imperialism: the policy or practice of extending a state's rule over other territories

infrastructure: underlying framework or features of a system or organization

Kyoto Protocol: an international agreement that aims to reduce carbon dioxide emissions and the presence of greenhouse gases

mandate: an authoritative command or instruction

manifesto: a public declaration of intentions, opinions, objectives, or motives

Medicare: Canada's national health insurance program

Meech Lake Accord: a set of constitutional reforms designed to induce Québec to accept the Constitution Act

minority government: a governing party that has half or fewer than half of the seats in the House of Commons or legislative assembly

one member one party voting system: electing party leaders or determining party policy by a direct vote of the members of each party

political left: parties that emphasize support for working people

political spectrum: a term used to refer to the differences in ideology between the major political parties

privatization: transfer of government services or assets to the private sector

Québec Referendum: a public vote to decide whether Québec should pursue a path toward sovereignty

responsible government: a form of government in which decisions cannot become law without the support of the majority of elected representatives

secede: to withdraw formally from membership in an organization, association, or alliance

socialism: an economic system in which the means of production, distribution, and exchange are owned by the community collectively, usually through the state

sovereigntist: someone who expresses support for making the province of Québec essentially independent from Canada

universal: including all members of a group

vote of non-confidence: a motion put before parliament to defeat or embarrass an opposing party

INDEX